The Trauma Bond Recovery Journal

The Trauma Bond Recovery Journal

12 weeks of reflection after a pathological love relationship

Lisa Sonni

To my baby bear Joey,

This book is dedicated to you, my brave little cub, who brought light into my life during the darkest times. You may never fully understand the depth of your impact on my life; I want you to know that you saved me in more ways than one. Your bright eyes and warm snuggles reminded me that there was still good in the world and that love and hope could conquer even the darkest moments. You gave me the strength to keep fighting, to never give up on myself, and to believe that a brighter future was possible for the three of us. May you always remember the power of love, both for yourself and others, and continue to bring light and hope to those around you.

Mummy

Contents

Lesson 1 Education

Week 1: Understanding your Trauma Bond
Week 2: Living in Reality
Week 3: Letting go of the Potential
Week 4: One Day at a Time

Lesson 2 Learn About Yourself

Week 5: Own Your Feelings
Week 6: Show Yourself Compassion
Week 7: Grieving The Loss
Week 8: Acceptable & Unacceptable Behaviors

Lesson 3 Build Your Future

Week 9: Your Unmet Needs
Week 10: Your Future Life
Week 11: Your Support System
Week 12: Self Love and Confidence

Trauma Bond Recovery Journal

Welcome to your recovery. Over the next 12 weeks for 5-10 minutes per day, you are going to take back control over your own life, work towards recovering from your trauma bond, and begin to really, truly love yourself again...or for the first time. Check out the **Trauma Bond Recovery Course**, my online self-guided program, and my second book in this series, **Rebuilding After A Trauma Bond: A Self-Love Journal.**

Lisa Sonni

Relationship & Recovery Coach
strongerthanbefore.ca

How To Use This Journal

This journal is set up for you to write 5 days a week over the span of 12 weeks, taking you through the trauma bond recovery stages. If you need longer, that's ok too. You will spend time reflecting on your relationship, as well as your innermost feelings and learn to build confidence. Never rush your recovery; it takes a different length of time for everyone. The key to your recovery is loving yourself so much that you no longer require validation from someone else.

This journal is best used in addition to trauma bond recovery coaching or therapy, as well as joining online support groups & educating yourself on trauma bonds.

Dig deep and really reflect on your answers when journaling to get the most out of your healing process.

Weekly Affirmations

Each week, there are three new affirmations. I like to do mine in the morning to start my day but you can do them at a time of day that works for you, but pick a consistent time. We all feel a bit silly talking to ourselves in the mirror. The more you tell yourself kind things, the more you believe them. Say these affirmations every day for the assigned week out loud ten times in a row. It only takes 2-3 minutes. Affirmations can change your mindset and help push negative thoughts out of your mind. Please feel free to add more of your own affirmations if you'd like. Find evidence in your life, past or present, that these affirmations are true for the best results.

Reflection Notes

Each week, you have space for reflection notes. Use this space to journal your feelings this week and any challenges you are feeling. Discuss in your coaching or therapy sessions.

What is a Trauma Bond?

A **trauma bond** is the result of ongoing cycles of abuse in which the sporadic reinforcement of positive reward and devaluation creates powerful emotional bonds that are incredibly resistant to change. Experts liken recovering from a trauma bond to a heroin addiction as there are both psychological and chemical factors that make recovery difficult.

. . . .

"A person can identify the patterns and become aware of the pathological dymanics inherent in the relationship".

Dr. Ramani
Clinical Psychologist

. . . .

7 Stages of a Trauma Bond

"Why can't I leave them?" is one of the most common questions we ask ourselves when in an abusive relationship. A trauma bond is very difficult to break. It helps to understand the stages of one to recognize and cope with the struggle you are having to walk away and feel good about your decision.

1. Love Bombing
The abuser showers you with love, kindness & validation to create an intense emotional bond. Promises and declarations of love are made.

2. Trust & Dependency
You start to rely on the abuser for emotional support and validation, believing that the abuser is the sole source of this comfort. They manipulate your emotions and create a cycle of intermittent reinforcement.

3. Devaluation
They reduce compliments and begin to criticize and belittle you to erode your self-worth. You may feel you deserve the mistreatment.

7 Stages of a Trauma Bond

4. Gaslighting

The abuser begins manipulating your perception of reality, causing you to question your own experiences and memories. You may feel isolated, which strengthens your reliance on the abuser.

5. Control

The abuser exerts dominance over you by dictating your actions, thoughts, and feelings. You are fully dependent by this stage and feel powerless.

6. Loss of Self

Your identity and sense of self become increasingly eroded due to ongoing abuse and manipulation. You may feel completely enmeshed with your abuser.

7. Addiction

You become emotionally and psychologically addicted to the cycle of abuse and intermittent reinforcement from your abuser. You will feel intense withdrawal symptoms if you attempt to separate.

Glossary of Terms

Here are some common words and phrases you will hear. For a complete guide, check out my book *Narcissism Unmasked: A Survivor's Handbook of the Common Narcissistic Abuse Tactics.*

Narcissistic Personality Disorder

A condition in which people have an inflated sense of their own importance, a deep need for excessive attention and admiration, abusive relationships, and a lack of empathy for others. There are 9 specific traits.

Narcissist

A person who may or may not hold the diagnosis of NPD, but displays narcissistic behavior and attitudes. Consider this a personality trait.

Hoovering

When the Narcissist is trying to suck you back into their life after you've left, they have discarded you, or you've shown them recent distance. This is their attempt to keep you in the relationship.

Gaslighting

This occurs when the Narcissist is trying to make you question yourself, your sanity and your memories. They will tell you that what you know is not true and what you saw does not exist.

Projection

A Narcissist will do this with traits about themselves that they hate, and use them to project onto you. They will accuse you of the things they are doing or call you the things they feel about themselves.

New Supply

This refers to the person your narcissist leaves you for, cheats on you with, or dates immediately following you.

Reactive Abuse

This occurs when the Narcissist has pushed you so hard and far that you react extremely out of character. They are typically there recording or will tell people that you are abusive and crazy as a result of this.

Empath

This is a common term used to describe the Narcissist's 'victim' because they are highly empathetic. Empath's are also typically kind, loyal & strong. They most often, but not always, have their own childhood trauma that needs to be healed. It is not a clinical term.

Enabler

This is a person who allows the Narcissist to behave this way, makes excuses for them, and does not question the Narcissist's version of things.

Flying Monkey

This name is inspired by Wizard of Oz, when the Flying Monkey's blindly support the Wicked Witch of the West's plans, regardless of how evil she is. Flying Monkey's offer blind loyalty and will typically attack the 'victim' on behalf of the Narcissist, ultimately participating in the abuse.

Future Faking

This is when a Narcissist will sell you the dream of the rest of your life, before you find yourself living the nightmare. Future faking can be as simple as "I will call you later" to "I want to marry you" or a more grandiose future.

Grey Rock

This is a term used to describe a low contact communication style with the Narcissist, in which you try to be "as boring as a rock" to train the Narcissist that you are no longer willing to engage in the drama & lies. A better method is BIFF (Brief, Informative, Firm, Friendly) and is better received in family court.

No Contact

This is the ideal situation with a Narcissist where they are completely and totally blocked and out of your life or have zero contact with you at all.

Mirroring

This most often occurs in the love bombing stage. A Narcissist struggles with real love & empathy so they mirror back to you what you are showing them.

Cognitive Dissonance

This refers to the mental discomfort and internal conflict experienced when your beliefs or values clash with the reality of your relationship. You are struggling to reconcile your love for them with the abuse you are suffering. To alleviate this discomfort, you rationalize, downplay, or blame yourself for the abuse. It results in perpetuating the abuse cycle.

• •

"It's better to conquer yourself than to win a thousand battles, then the victory is yours and it cannot be taken from you."

Buddha

• •

Week 1

Understanding Your Trauma Bond

"And after thinking you will never recover, that you will never get up off the floor again, you have dusted yourself off and carried on".

Nikita Gill

Affirmations

I am enough.

I am worthy of love.

Today, I choose me.

Week 1: Day 1

• •

What reasons have I identified or used to justify being in the relationship? Are these reasons truly rational?

_____

_____

_____

_____

_____

_____

_____

_____

_____

_____

_____

_____

_____

_____

_____

_____

_____

_____

_____

_____

_____

_____

_____

Week 1: Day 2

What did or does my partner tell me about our future together? Do I believe it?

_____
_____
_____
_____
_____
_____
_____
_____
_____
_____
_____
_____
_____
_____
_____
_____
_____
_____
_____
_____
_____
_____
_____
_____
_____
_____

Week 1: Day 3

Has my partner made me aware of any of their childhood traumas which makes me want to be their saviour? Was saving them ever realistic?

_____

_____

_____

_____

_____

_____

_____

_____

_____

_____

_____

_____

_____

_____

_____

_____

_____

_____

_____

_____

_____

_____

_____

_____

Week 1: Day 4

What expectations have I placed on myself that may contribute to challenges or delays in leaving the relationship?

_____
_____
_____
_____
_____
_____
_____
_____
_____
_____
_____
_____
_____
_____
_____
_____
_____
_____
_____
_____
_____
_____
_____
_____
_____

Week 1: Day 5

What did I really feel inside when my partner devalued & criticized me? How has this affected my self worth?

_____
_____
_____
_____
_____
_____
_____
_____
_____
_____
_____
_____
_____
_____
_____
_____
_____
_____
_____
_____
_____
_____
_____
_____
_____

Week 1: Reflection Notes

Week 2

Living in Reality

"You'll never be able to create the right reality if you're not willing to let the wrong reality go".

Lolly Daskal

Affirmations

I overcome challenges with ease.

I believe in myself.

I let go of that which no longer serves me.

Week 2: Day 1

What childhood traumas of mine, up to age 6, do I need to heal? How did my parents or caregivers make me feel? How does that impact me now?

_____
_____
_____
_____
_____
_____
_____
_____
_____
_____
_____
_____
_____
_____
_____
_____
_____
_____
_____
_____
_____
_____
_____
_____
_____
_____
_____
_____

Week 2: Day 2

What have I, as an empath or people pleaser, contributed to this cycle of abuse?

_____
_____
_____
_____
_____
_____
_____
_____
_____
_____
_____
_____
_____
_____
_____
_____
_____
_____
_____
_____
_____
_____
_____
_____

Week 2: Day 3

What fears of mine have gotten in the way of ending this toxic cycle of abuse?

_____
_____
_____
_____
_____
_____
_____
_____
_____
_____
_____
_____
_____
_____
_____
_____
_____
_____
_____
_____
_____
_____
_____
_____
_____

Week 2: Day 4

· ·

What are my strengths that will help me build a
better future without them? List at least 4.

_____
_____
_____
_____
_____
_____
_____
_____
_____
_____
_____
_____
_____
_____
_____
_____
_____
_____
_____
_____
_____
_____
_____
_____

Week 2: Day 5

What biases do I have that contributed to me staying in this cycle?

_____

_____

_____

_____

_____

_____

_____

_____

_____

_____

_____

_____

_____

_____

_____

_____

_____

_____

_____

_____

_____

_____

_____

_____

_____

_____

Week 2: Reflection Notes

_____
_____
_____
_____
_____
_____
_____
_____
_____
_____
_____
_____
_____
_____
_____
_____
_____
_____
_____
_____
_____
_____
_____
_____

Letting Go of the Potential

"Closure happens right after you accept that letting go and moving on is more important than projecting a fantasy of how the relationship could have been".

Sylvester McNutt

Affirmations

I no longer fear the unknown.

I choose to focus only on what I can control.

I choose to be optimistic.

Week 3: Day 1

What future did we plan & dream of together? Was it obtainable based on their actions?

_____
_____
_____
_____
_____
_____
_____
_____
_____
_____
_____
_____
_____
_____
_____
_____
_____
_____
_____
_____
_____
_____
_____

Week 3: Day 2

What future do I want or can I have for myself without them? What are *my* dreams & goals?

_____
_____
_____
_____
_____
_____
_____
_____
_____
_____
_____
_____
_____
_____
_____
_____
_____
_____
_____
_____
_____
_____
_____
_____
_____
_____

Week 3: Day 3

What beliefs do I have that are limiting my own potential to move on? Are these facts or beliefs?

_____

_____

_____

_____

_____

_____

_____

_____

_____

_____

_____

_____

_____

_____

_____

_____

_____

_____

_____

_____

_____

_____

_____

_____

_____

_____

Week 3: Day 4

How can I use my experience in this relationship to push myself forward? What have I learned?

_____
_____
_____
_____
_____
_____
_____
_____
_____
_____
_____
_____
_____
_____
_____
_____
_____
_____
_____
_____
_____
_____
_____
_____
_____
_____

Week 3: Day 5

What did they tell me about themselves that I believed but I know now are not true? How do I know they are not true?

_____
_____
_____
_____
_____
_____
_____
_____
_____
_____
_____
_____
_____
_____
_____
_____
_____
_____
_____
_____
_____
_____
_____
_____

Week 3: Reflection Notes

_____
_____
_____
_____
_____
_____
_____
_____
_____
_____
_____
_____
_____
_____
_____
_____
_____
_____
_____
_____
_____
_____
_____
_____
_____
_____
_____
_____
_____
_____

Letting Go of the Potential

Week 4

One Day at a Time

""There will be bad days. Be calm. Loosen your grip, opening each palm slowly now. Let go. Be confident".

Shane Koyczan

Affirmations

I know who I am and what I deserve.

My past does not define my future.

I have the power to create the life I desire.

Week 4: Day 1

What are 2 or more things I can do today that will bring me closer to my end goal of breaking the trauma bond?

_____

_____

_____

_____

_____

_____

_____

_____

_____

_____

_____

_____

_____

_____

_____

_____

_____

_____

_____

_____

_____

Week 4: Day 2

When did I last push the boundaries of my comfort zone? How did I feel when I did?

_____
_____
_____
_____
_____
_____
_____
_____
_____
_____
_____
_____
_____
_____
_____
_____
_____
_____
_____
_____
_____
_____
_____
_____

Week 4: Day 3

What is a recent slip up I've had that I need to forgive myself for? How can I show myself forgiveness?

_____
_____
_____
_____
_____
_____
_____
_____
_____
_____
_____
_____
_____
_____
_____
_____
_____
_____
_____
_____
_____
_____
_____
_____
_____
_____

Week 4: Day 4

What are the negative thoughts I need to work on pushing out of my mind? What can I replace them with?

_____

_____

_____

_____

_____

_____

_____

_____

_____

_____

_____

_____

_____

_____

_____

_____

_____

_____

_____

_____

_____

_____

_____

_____

_____

Week 4: Day 5

If this were the last day of my life, would I have the same plans for today? What would I do instead?

_____

_____

_____

_____

_____

_____

_____

_____

_____

_____

_____

_____

_____

_____

_____

_____

_____

_____

_____

_____

_____

_____

_____

_____

_____

Week 4: Reflection Notes

How Are You Doing So Far?

Keep pushing forward. I know how hard it is to heal from the trauma bond. You are waking up every day and choosing yourself. You are taking the right steps. Self reflection, being *radically* honest with yourself and introspection will carry you through the next 8 weeks of this journal. Don't stop.

• •

"Sometimes it takes a heartbreak to shake us awake & help us see we are worth so much more than we are settling for".

Mandy Hale

• •

Week 5

Own Your Feelings

"It took letting go to realize I was holding on to nothing".

R. H. Shin

Affirmations

I am in control.

I am stronger than my excuses.

I am unaffected by the judgement of others.

Week 5: Day 1

How did I feel about myself before I ever met them? At what point in my life did I feel my best?

_____
_____
_____
_____
_____
_____
_____
_____
_____
_____
_____
_____
_____
_____
_____
_____
_____
_____
_____
_____
_____
_____
_____
_____
_____
_____

Week 5: Day 2

Many feelings mask themselves as anger. What do I really feel, rather than anger? How does anger hold me back from healing?

_____

_____

_____

_____

_____

_____

_____

_____

_____

_____

_____

_____

_____

_____

_____

_____

_____

_____

_____

_____

_____

_____

_____

_____

_____

Week 5: Day 3

How can I reflect on a time that I lost control to better manage how I react in the future?

_____
_____
_____
_____
_____
_____
_____
_____
_____
_____
_____
_____
_____
_____
_____
_____
_____
_____
_____
_____
_____
_____
_____
_____
_____
_____
_____

Week 5: Day 4

What societal norms do I allow in my mind that make me bottle up or hide my emotions?

_____
_____
_____
_____
_____
_____
_____
_____
_____
_____
_____
_____
_____
_____
_____
_____
_____
_____
_____
_____
_____
_____
_____
_____
_____
_____

Week 5: Day 5

What are the ways in which I let them have control over my own feelings? What can I do to own my own feelings?

_____

_____

_____

_____

_____

_____

_____

_____

_____

_____

_____

_____

_____

_____

_____

_____

_____

_____

_____

_____

_____

_____

_____

_____

Own Your Feelings

Week 5: Reflection Notes

Week 6

Show Yourself Compassion

"Having compassion starts and ends with having compassion for all those unwanted parts of ourselves".

Pema Chodron

Affirmations

I don't fail. I learn.

I forgive myself for accepting this abuse in the past and I can move forward.

My setbacks redirect me to something bigger & better.

Week 6: Day 1

How can I positively reframe the way I think about myself? What are my own perceived weaknesses that could actually be strengths?

_____

_____

_____

_____

_____

_____

_____

_____

_____

_____

_____

_____

_____

_____

_____

_____

_____

_____

_____

Week 6: Day 2

What are specific things I am struggling to forgive myself for? Am I being too self-critical?

_____
_____
_____
_____
_____
_____
_____
_____
_____
_____
_____
_____
_____
_____
_____
_____
_____
_____
_____
_____
_____
_____
_____
_____
_____

Week 6: Day 3

What are 2-3 actions can I take to let go of my need for external validation?

_____

_____

_____

_____

_____

_____

_____

_____

_____

_____

_____

_____

_____

_____

_____

_____

_____

_____

_____

_____

_____

_____

_____

_____

_____

Week 6: Day 4

· ·

What are 3-5 things I see as flaws in myself that I
can start to accept & embrace?

_____

_____

_____

_____

_____

_____

_____

_____

_____

_____

_____

_____

_____

_____

_____

_____

_____

_____

_____

_____

_____

_____

_____

_____

_____

Week 6: Day 5

What are some things in my life and about myself that I am grateful for? I will list as many as I can.

_____

_____

_____

_____

_____

_____

_____

_____

_____

_____

_____

_____

_____

_____

_____

_____

_____

_____

_____

_____

_____

_____

_____

Week 6: Reflection Notes

Week 7

Grieving The Loss

"Grief is not a disorder, a disease or a sign of weakness. The only cure for grief is to grieve".

Earl Grollman

Affirmations

Today and every day I choose to be happy.

I am resilient.

All that I need comes to me at the right time.

Week 7: Day 1

How am I truly feeling about the loss of my potential life and future that I envisioned?

_____
_____
_____
_____
_____
_____
_____
_____
_____
_____
_____
_____
_____
_____
_____
_____
_____
_____
_____
_____
_____
_____
_____
_____
_____
_____

Week 7: Day 2

How can I ask the people around me for support through my grief, whether they understand what I am feeling or not? What do I need?

_____
_____
_____
_____
_____
_____
_____
_____
_____
_____
_____
_____
_____
_____
_____
_____
_____
_____
_____
_____
_____
_____
_____
_____
_____

Week 7: Day 3

What judgements am I making of myself for feeling grief due to the loss of my relationship with my abuser that I need to let go of?

_____

_____

_____

_____

_____

_____

_____

_____

_____

_____

_____

_____

_____

_____

_____

_____

_____

_____

_____

_____

_____

_____

Week 7: Day 4

Who am I without this person? What is my potential? What am I capable of?

_____
_____
_____
_____
_____
_____
_____
_____
_____
_____
_____
_____
_____
_____
_____
_____
_____
_____
_____
_____
_____
_____
_____

Week 7: Day 5

· ·

What do I want to say to my abuser about how
they have made me feel?

_____
_____
_____
_____
_____
_____
_____
_____
_____
_____
_____
_____
_____
_____
_____
_____
_____
_____
_____
_____
_____
_____
_____
_____
_____
_____

Week 7: Reflection Notes

_____
_____
_____
_____
_____
_____
_____
_____
_____
_____
_____
_____
_____
_____
_____
_____
_____
_____
_____
_____
_____
_____
_____
_____
_____

Week 8

Acceptable & Unacceptable Behaviors

"Some of the bravest things you can do are say 'no' and set boundaries when you spent a lifetime convinced that you needed to please others in order to be loved."

Xavier Dagba

Affirmations

I don't need to accept every invitation to an argument.

I can respect the feelings of others and still honor my own.

I don't need permission to follow my own heart.

Week 8: Day 1

What were/are the top areas of concern with my abusive relationship? Why are these areas concerning to me?

_____

_____

_____

_____

_____

_____

_____

_____

_____

_____

_____

_____

_____

_____

_____

_____

_____

_____

_____

_____

_____

_____

_____

_____

Acceptable & Unacceptable Behaviors

Week 8: Day 2

What are 5 unacceptable behaviors from my abuser? How do/did these behaviors make me feel about myself?

_____
_____
_____
_____
_____
_____
_____
_____
_____
_____
_____
_____
_____
_____
_____
_____
_____
_____
_____
_____
_____
_____
_____

Week 8: Day 3

What are the behaviors of a loving person that I would value most? How do I anticipate they would make me feel?

_____
_____
_____
_____
_____
_____
_____
_____
_____
_____
_____
_____
_____
_____
_____
_____
_____
_____
_____
_____
_____
_____
_____

Week 8: Day 4

What are some bottom line behaviors for me?
E.g. "I will not argue with someone who has been drinking".

_____

_____

_____

_____

_____

_____

_____

_____

_____

_____

_____

_____

_____

_____

_____

_____

_____

_____

_____

_____

_____

_____

_____

Acceptable & Unacceptable Behaviors

Week 8: Day 5

In the future, how will I approach it if I see an unacceptable behavior? How will I feel, and how will I express myself?

_____
_____
_____
_____
_____
_____
_____
_____
_____
_____
_____
_____
_____
_____
_____
_____
_____
_____
_____
_____
_____
_____
_____
_____
_____

Week 8: Reflection Notes

Acceptable & Unacceptable Behaviors

You Can Do This

In a trauma bond, you have been conditioned to think you cannot be without him/her, to think you are not good enough, to think you have little to no value. You can reframe your thoughts. You can replace those feelings of self doubt and learn to love yourself so much that validation from him/her will no longer hold weight in your life.

Your next step is to order the next journal in my series, **Rebuilding After A Trauma Bond: A Self-Love Journal,** so you can continue healing and rebuild your sense of self.

• •

"You alone are enough. You have nothing to prove to anybody."

Maya Angelou

• •

Week 9

Your Unmet Needs

"Your greatest responsibility is to love yourself and to know you are enough."

Chetna Mishra

Affirmations

Everything I need is within me.

I can ask for what I want & need.

I prioritize myself and my needs.

Week 9: Day 1

When I feel/felt angry at my abuser, what is it that I really need(ed)? What was/am I longing for?

_____
_____
_____
_____
_____
_____
_____
_____
_____
_____
_____
_____
_____
_____
_____
_____
_____
_____
_____
_____
_____
_____
_____
_____

Week 9: Day 2

When my abuser has ignored my requests, what did that action represent to me? How did I feel?

_____
_____
_____
_____
_____
_____
_____
_____
_____
_____
_____
_____
_____
_____
_____
_____
_____
_____
_____
_____
_____
_____
_____
_____
_____
_____
_____

Week 9: Day 3

What promises did my abuser make to me that I felt met a need of mine? How did I feel at the possibility of having this need met?

_____
_____
_____
_____
_____
_____
_____
_____
_____
_____
_____
_____
_____
_____
_____
_____
_____
_____
_____
_____
_____
_____
_____
_____
_____
_____

Week 9: Day 4

How do I feel at the thought of this relationship never being the one that will meet my needs?

_____
_____
_____
_____
_____
_____
_____
_____
_____
_____
_____
_____
_____
_____
_____
_____
_____
_____
_____
_____
_____
_____
_____
_____
_____
_____

Week 9: Day 5

What are my own emotional needs? Which of them can I meet myself?

_____
_____
_____
_____
_____
_____
_____
_____
_____
_____
_____
_____
_____
_____
_____
_____
_____
_____
_____
_____
_____
_____
_____
_____

Week 9: Reflection Notes

_____
_____
_____
_____
_____
_____
_____
_____
_____
_____
_____
_____
_____
_____
_____
_____
_____
_____
_____
_____
_____
_____
_____
_____
_____
_____

Your Unmet Needs

Week 10

Your Future Life

"Look closely at the present you are constructing. It should look like the future you are dreaming."

Alice Walker

Affirmations

I live from this moment forwards.

My possibilities are endless.

My future has a purpose and will exceed my expectations.

Week 10: Day 1

What are my professional goals? Am I happy with
what I am doing? What would fulfill me?

_____
_____
_____
_____
_____
_____
_____
_____
_____
_____
_____
_____
_____
_____
_____
_____
_____
_____
_____
_____
_____
_____
_____
_____

Week 10: Day 2

What dreams did I have before I met my abuser that I have not fulfilled? Do I still want this or do I have new dreams? What are they?

_____
_____
_____
_____
_____
_____
_____
_____
_____
_____
_____
_____
_____
_____
_____
_____
_____
_____
_____
_____
_____
_____
_____
_____

Week 10: Day 3

What would a weekend completely alone look like? Would I enjoy that? Why or why not? Am I comfortable alone?

_____

_____

_____

_____

_____

_____

_____

_____

_____

_____

_____

_____

_____

_____

_____

_____

_____

_____

_____

_____

_____

_____

_____

_____

_____

Week 10: Day 4

What are 2 life affirming choices I can make, free from my toxic relationship, that will make me feel happy?

_____

_____

_____

_____

_____

_____

_____

_____

_____

_____

_____

_____

_____

_____

_____

_____

_____

_____

_____

_____

_____

_____

Week 10: Day 5

What are hobbies I can learn/activities I can do/clubs I can join to build a new life for myself? Is this outside of my comfort zone?

_____
_____
_____
_____
_____
_____
_____
_____
_____
_____
_____
_____
_____
_____
_____
_____
_____
_____
_____
_____
_____
_____
_____
_____
_____

Week 10: Reflection Notes

Your Support System

"Anything is possible when you have the right people there to support you."

Misty Copeland

Affirmations

I have (or will build) a healthy support system.

I will lean on (or find & join) an online support group of people who have experienced what I have.

I am my own best friend.

Week 11: Day 1

What type of support do I need? Financial/emotional/physical or a combination? What does this support look like to me?

_____

_____

_____

_____

_____

_____

_____

_____

_____

_____

_____

_____

_____

_____

_____

_____

_____

_____

_____

_____

Week 11: Day 2

Is there anyone in my support system that I should remove because I don't feel supported? What are traits to avoid when creating my support system?

_____
_____
_____
_____
_____
_____
_____
_____
_____
_____
_____
_____
_____
_____
_____
_____
_____
_____
_____
_____
_____
_____
_____

Week 11: Day 3

Who did I or do I have the healthiest relationships with? How can I reconnect or increase my connection with this person or someone like them?

_____
_____
_____
_____
_____
_____
_____
_____
_____
_____
_____
_____
_____
_____
_____
_____
_____
_____
_____
_____
_____
_____

Week 11: Day 4

Are there any excuses I am making that prevent support I am being offered? Have I truly done everything I can to find support in my life, including not for profit resources if applicable?

_____
_____
_____
_____
_____
_____
_____
_____
_____
_____
_____
_____
_____
_____
_____
_____
_____
_____
_____
_____
_____
_____

Your Support System

Week 11: Day 5

Have I considered hiring a coach or therapist? (Have I considered not for profit options?) Could I befriend someone online in a support group? Who can I get deep with?

_____

_____

_____

_____

_____

_____

_____

_____

_____

_____

_____

_____

_____

_____

_____

_____

_____

_____

_____

_____

_____

_____

Your Support System

Week 11: Reflection Notes

Week 12

Self Love & Confidence

"If you are searching for that one person who will change your life, take a look in the mirror."

Ernest Holmes

Affirmations

No matter what I've done or not done, I am worthy of love.

I am perfect just as I am.

I am always enough.

I love my _____ (insert feature you feel a bit insecure about)

I am strong & capable.

Week 12: Day 1

Do I compare myself to others, and if so, in what ways? How is this harmful? How can I focus on myself more?

Week 12: Day 2

What do I believe about the concept of self love? What I have been taught about displaying confidence?

_____

_____

_____

_____

_____

_____

_____

_____

_____

_____

_____

_____

_____

_____

_____

_____

_____

_____

_____

_____

_____

_____

_____

_____

Week 12: Day 3

How can I start to put myself first? Will I feel good about it? Why or why not? Why is this self love?

_____

_____

_____

_____

_____

_____

_____

_____

_____

_____

_____

_____

_____

_____

_____

_____

_____

_____

_____

_____

_____

_____

_____

_____

Week 12: Day 4

What and who am I holding onto that isn't serving me anymore? How does this affect my future and my healing?

_____
_____
_____
_____
_____
_____
_____
_____
_____
_____
_____
_____
_____
_____
_____
_____
_____
_____
_____
_____
_____
_____

Week 12: Day 5

How can I/do I make myself feel better? How can
I make myself BE better? What are the actions I
can take or behaviors I can change?

_____
_____
_____
_____
_____
_____
_____
_____
_____
_____
_____
_____
_____
_____
_____
_____
_____
_____
_____
_____
_____
_____
_____
_____
_____

Week 12: Reflection Notes

Emotions When Breaking a Trauma Bond

When an abusive relationship ends, you are going to feel grief, regardless of the relationship being abusive or toxic. You are grieving a life that you dreamt of, the loss of the potential for your future. With grief comes sadness, anger, anxiety and/or depression and feelings of withdrawal. It is important to let yourself feel your feelings.

Anger is not where you want to land. Anger is part of the process, but the end goal is to feel *indifference* towards the narcissist. Anger means you have not healed and you still have 'big feelings' to work through. This anger has often been referred to as righteous anger because it feels so justified.

Your next step in healing might just be my **Rebuilding After A Trauma Bond: A Self-Love Journal.** So let's get into loving yourself and what that means.

Learning how to love yourself, set boundaries, and put yourself first is a choice that you have made by using this journal. That is an excellent first step in healing and educating yourself. You are **stronger than before.** Don't stop.

• •

"Your trauma is valid. Even if other people have experienced "worse". Even if someone else who went through the same experience doesn't feel debilitated by it. Even if it "could have been avoided". Even if it happened a long time ago. Even if no one knows. Your trauma is real and valid and you deserve a space to talk about it. It isn't desperate or pathetic or attention-seeking. It's self-care. It's *inconceivably* brave. And regardless of the magnitude of your struggle, you're allowed to take care of yourself by processing and unloading some of the pain you carry. Your pain matters. Your experience matters. And your healing matters. Nothing and no one can take that away." Daniell Koepke

Made in the USA
Las Vegas, NV
22 October 2024

10330134R00062